The Research Paper

The Research Paper

McDougal, Littell & Company

Evanston, Illinois

New York   Dallas   Sacramento   Raleigh

This book is the result of many years' experience in teaching high school students how to write a research paper. The success of the procedure has been substantiated by teachers and students who have used it. The style for documentation and bibliography has been distilled from *The MLA Style Manual* and *The MLA Handbook for Writers of Research Papers.* We hope the book works successfully for you.

ISBN 0-86609-346-X

94 95 96 97 98 99 / 10 9 8 7 6

Contents

Part 1

Understanding the Research Paper

By this time in high school, you have probably had to write a research paper in one of your classes. A research paper is an in-depth study in which the writer investigates, analyzes, and evaluates a specific problem or question that is related to a wider issue. The issue may be historical, political, social, literary, or scientific. Following are some possible subjects for a research paper:

Does the Media's Coverage of Candidates Affect Voters' Opinions?
Is There a Link Between Nutrition and Mental Health?
How the Women's Movement Changed the American Work Force

Two critical qualities distinguish the research paper from an ordinary composition. First, the research paper is longer—between ten and twenty pages. Second, the research paper is more formal and requires research into reliable sources.

There is more to writing a good research paper, however, than presenting research findings. As mentioned earlier, your research paper will be based on a problem or a question. For the subject of media coverage of candidates, for example, the question could be whether negative coverage of a candidate has the same effect as positive coverage. In "solving the problem" of your paper, you exercise your own thinking as you mold your information into a solution.

This book will take you through the step-by-step process of writing a research paper. These steps are as follows:

1. Choose and limit your subject.
2. Prepare a working bibliography.
3. Read and take notes.
4. Organize your notes and write the final outline.
5. Write the first draft.
6. Revise the first draft.
7. Write the final draft with documentation.
8. Write the final bibliography.

Writing a research paper is an ambitious task; however, the basic steps involved are quite similar to those you have learned for writing any composition. If you follow the guidelines in this book and apply what you have already learned about writing compositions, your research paper can prove to be an extremely rewarding assignment.

Approaches to Research

While conducting the research for your paper, you may take two basic approaches. In one approach, involving **primary research,** you gather your own information. There are a number of ways to accomplish this. For a science research paper, you might perform a series of experiments. For a social science paper, you might conduct a personal interview. One history student, interested in the early small towns of New England, used the resources of a historical library that stored the official records of many of these towns, including records of births, deaths, marriages, land purchases, and elections. Once you complete such primary research, you analyze your information and present your findings.

Most of your research papers, however, will involve a different approach, entailing **secondary research.** In doing secondary research, you gather and analyze facts and ideas from published sources such as books and articles.

Some topics can be approached through either primary or secondary research. Look at the following research topic, for example.

Television: Its Effects on Preschool Children

A primary study of this issue could, for example, involve interviews with parents of preschool children or observations of the children themselves as they watch television and afterwards. Secondary research, in contrast, would require the writer to find published books and articles on the topic in reputable sources. Remember, however, that a paper based on secondary research may sometimes be improved with the addition of some primary research.

The Structure of the Research Paper

Whether your research is primary or secondary, the resulting paper needs to have a certain basic structure. This structure begins with an introduction in which you present your problem or question and explain your method of handling it. Next comes the core of your paper—a series of body paragraphs that develop your main idea with details from authoritative sources. After the body paragraphs you write a conclusion explaining what you have found in your research and analysis and the implications of your findings. Throughout your paper, you must provide complete documentation of all sources you have used. Finally, at the end of your paper, you must present a complete bibliography that lists these sources.

Writing Activity   The Research Paper

Explain how you might do both a primary and a secondary research paper for each of the following topics. Tell what sources of information you might use.

> Is Child Abuse Running Rampant in American Society?
> How Effective Is Advertising?
> Are Space Colonies on the Moon the Frontiers of the Future?
> America's Homeless: What Are the Solutions?

Part 2

Planning the Research Paper

In order to use your time wisely and efficiently, you need to plan your research paper carefully. Choosing and limiting your topic is the first important step in planning your paper.

Choosing a Topic

The following guidelines will help you choose a topic for your research paper.

1. **Choose a subject that interests you.** Choose a subject that you want to learn more about. If your subject does not really interest you, your paper will probably not interest the reader either.

2. **Choose a subject for which a wide range of source materials is readily available.** Subjects that are too recent in development, or too technical in nature, will have few, if any, source materials. If you have doubts about source materials for a subject, consult your school librarian to find out how much information the library has. Also check the card or computer catalog listings, the vertical file, and the *Readers' Guide to Periodical Literature.*

3. **Choose a subject of some significance.** A subject of lasting interest will be challenging and gratifying to pursue. After all, you will be spending much time and effort on this assignment, and what you learn should be a significant addition to your store of knowledge as well as that of the reader.

4. **Choose a subject that can be presented objectively.** Your purpose is to sift through and reshape an accumulated body of information, not to indulge in argument and persuasion. Argument and persuasion are right for debates, but not for a research paper. Your paper should be an objective presentation.

5. **Avoid straight biography.** Biography requires long intensive research, involving letters, interviews, and unpublished material not available to the average person. If the person is well known, biographies already exist and using them as resource material, even if they are in unusual quantity, results merely in a rehashing of already published information. If you do wish to write about some interesting figure, try to choose an unusual angle or viewpoint.

Limiting a Topic

Limiting the scope of your chosen topic is the next step in the planning of a research paper. Since your paper will probably number from ten to twenty pages, you need to limit your topic so that it can be fully covered in the space available.

One way to begin limiting your subject is to do some general reading in reference works. By doing this, you can learn what topics lie within the broader subject that you have chosen. Encyclopedias, magazines, almanacs, biographical reference works, and literary reference works are useful for this purpose. In addition to consulting reference sources, you may wish to glance at indexes or tables of contents in books on your subject. These will show you how other people have broken down the subject in the past.

When limiting your subject, bear in mind that your paper should serve a definite purpose. The purpose may be to inform your audience about a topic, to analyze the topic, or to compare or contrast one topic with another. Keeping a specific purpose in mind will help you to narrow the topic before beginning your research. Having a definite purpose may also provide an interesting angle or approach to the actual writing of the paper.

Consider the wide variety of possible topics for an American Studies research paper—from the effects of television on children to Vietnam veterans in today's society. An interesting subject of American Studies has always been the Civil War. As you read the topics below, notice how one student limited the scope of a topic on the Civil War.

One Student's Process
1. The Civil War
2. Common soldiers of the Civil War
3. The experience of the common soldier in the Civil War

The third topic is limited in scope but it needs more focus for a 2,000-word (ten to twelve pages) paper. Since there is a great deal of literature written about the Civil War, and since American Studies combines literature and history, the writer developed this topic:

One Student's Process
Determine whether Stephen Crane's <u>The Red Badge of Courage</u> accurately depicts the experiences of the common soldier in the Civil War through the novel's protagonist, Henry Fleming.

Limiting a Topic

1. Do some general reading on your topic in an encyclopedia or other reference book. You may also want to scan the indexes or tables of contents of some books on the topic.
2. Establish the purpose of your paper.
3. Be sure that your topic can be handled in the space available, usually about ten to twenty pages.
4. Focus on a particular aspect of your topic that will lend itself to a wide variety of source materials.

Writing Activity   Planning the Research Paper

Decide on a topic for a research paper. If you need help, choose one from the list below. Limit your topic so that it meets the criteria described in the box above and is suitable for a ten- to twenty-page research paper. In later activities you will develop a research paper for your limited topic.

Probing Other Planets: Venus, Mercury, and Mars
The History of Photography
The Analysis of Dreams
Nuclear Power: Fission vs. Fusion

Part 3

Beginning Your Research

Once you have limited a topic and your teacher has approved it, you are ready to begin your research. The process of research includes a number of steps—locating, analyzing, evaluating, and employing information from a variety of reliable sources. Your next step is to indentify useful sources of information for your paper.

Identifying Sources

As you search for sources, you will be compiling a **working bibliography**—a list of potentially useful materials for your research paper. Begin your search by consulting reference works, such as encyclopedias, that contain entries on your general subject. You can also check the *Readers' Guide to Periodical Literature* to find articles that deal with your subject in a general way. Consulting such reference works will give you an overview of the subject. It may also suggest possible modifications in the subject you have chosen. (If you do decide to modify your subject, consult your teacher.)

At this point, you may wish to review the primary sources for your research so that you can use your library time wisely. The following sources are the most important for a research paper.

1. **The card catalog** Suppose you are doing a paper on the writing style of William Faulkner. You would first look at all the subject cards or computer entries listed under his name. In addition to all the books Faulkner has written, you will find major biographies and works of criticism mainly concerned with him.

   However, many books that may have informative chapters on Faulkner may not be entered under the heading *Faulkner*. Therefore, you should also look at "American Literature," "Twentieth-Century Literature," "Literature of the South," "The Novel," "Literary Criticism," and any other general subjects related to Faulkner and his work. The short description of the book on the card will tell you whether the book is worth investigating.

2. **The *Readers' Guide to Periodical Literature*** This source will list current magazine articles on your subject. For many subjects, past articles are as useful as present ones, and the library has cumulative, bound volumes of past years.

3. **Specialized reference books** In the reference section of your library you will find reference works on general and specific subjects. See whether any relate to your subject. They often suggest additional books that may be useful. One type of reference work that may be helpful is called a bibliography. It lists the research, books, and articles about a given subject. There are two types of bibliographies. An **annual bibliography** lists all the material written about a topic in a specific year, while a **general bibliography** provides a more extensive list of sources. Such bibliographies can tell you what has already been written on your topic. To locate these reference books, consult the subject and title heading *Bibliography* in the card catalog.

4. **Other sources** Do not neglect interviews, television programs, radio shows, recordings, graphic aids, and other possible sources of information. These often provide unique insights that can add considerably to the freshness of a paper.

In preparing a working bibliography, your objective is to accumulate as many books and articles as you think might be helpful. Because you cannot always tell whether the information on a catalog card or in the *Readers' Guide* or in a bibliography will be worthwhile, it is wise to include sources you may be doubtful about at the moment. If some sources turn out to be of little help, you can later drop them from your bibliography.

Evaluating Potential Sources

After you have listed and located your potential sources, you need to decide how useful each will be to your paper. Such evaluation is a key step, since it will determine the quality of your information.

As you evaluate your sources, keep in mind that each source can be useful in two ways. First, it may provide a general background or summary of the topic. Reading such a source may improve your understanding of the topic, suggest methods of organizing your paper, or lead you to additional sources. Second, a particular source may help you to support, illustrate, or even refute a specific point or argument. The following guidelines will help you evaluate your sources.

Selecting Source Materials

1. Is the author an authority on the subject? While you may not know this at the beginning, an author who has written several books on your subject or whose name is included in various bibliographies may be an authoritative source.

2. Is the source reliable, unbiased, and up-to-date? A book on a well-known politician, written by a friend or relative, may not be as accurate as one written by an authority on politics. A book on computers published in 1968 may not be as accurate as one published in 1989. A third edition of a book would be more valuable than the first or second edition. Recent material is very important for topics that have ongoing research.

3. If a magazine article looks promising, what kind of magazine does it appear in? Many popular interest magazines are not suitable sources for a research paper.

4. If a book looks promising, for what audience is it intended? Many interesting books are really intended for younger readers. Because they present information in an overly simplified form, they are not suitable for research papers. Books of a highly technical nature are also usually unsuitable. They are too detailed and too complex for the average reader.

5. Are additional books or articles included in any of the bibliographies you have consulted? You may be able to find bibliographies in many of the books listed in the card catalog. When you find one, examine its entries closely. If the same books or authors appear in several bibliographies, they are probably worth investigating.

Preparing Bibliography Cards

On a 3" x 5" index card or slip of paper, record each bibliography source you decide to use for your paper. Be sure to fill out your bibliography cards carefully and completely, so that they will effectively serve these three basic purposes:

1. To enable you to find the reference in the library
2. To enable you to prepare the documentation for your paper
3. To help you prepare the final bibliography for your paper

Following are the correct forms for bibliography cards from three different kinds of sources: a book, a magazine, and an encyclopedia.

See the box on page 25 for more information you may need to include.

Book

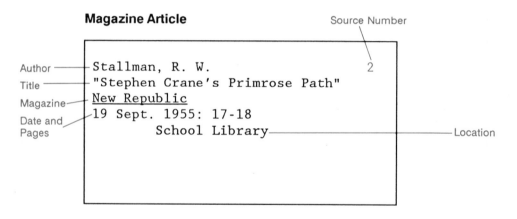

Source Number

Author —————	Catton, Bruce 1
Title —————	This Hallowed Ground
Publishing ————	New York: Doubleday, 1956
Information	
Call Number	973.7 Public Library ————————— Location

Magazine Article

Source Number

Author ————	Stallman, R. W. 2
Title ————	"Stephen Crane's Primrose Path"
Magazine ——	New Republic
Date and	19 Sept. 1955: 17-18
Pages	School Library ———————— Location

Encyclopedia Article

Source Number

Title ————	"Civil War" 3
Reference ——	World Book Encyclopedia
Date ——	1986 ed.
Call Number	Ref AE
	5
	W.55 School Library ————————— Location

The following additional information will be helpful in preparing bibliography cards.

1. When you first locate a source, find the correct bibliography entries on pages 26-28. Then write a bibliography card, making certain that you include all the necessary information.
2. If a book has an editor rather than an author, use *ed.* (editor) or *eds.* (editors) after the name: Bloom, Harold, ed.
3. Published works italicize book titles and names of periodicals. To signify italics when using a typewriter, underline these words.
4. If no publication date is given, use the copyright date.
5. If neither publication nor copyright date is given, use the abbreviation *n.d.* (no date).
6. Publication information is usually found on the title page. Sometimes pamphlets carry this information on front or back covers or on the last page. Magazines may have the information on the front cover or on one of the first pages.
7. The source number in the upper right-hand corner of your card will save you time when you are writing your first draft. Instead of having to write out all the bibliographic information every time you use the source, you can merely jot down the number of the card. Later, use these numbers to locate the cards.

Writing Activity Beginning Your Research

Compile a working bibliography for the topic you chose in Part 2. Use at least seven sources, including several books, at least two articles, and one reference source.

Part 4

Taking Notes

Once you have collected and recorded your source materials, you are ready to begin taking notes. To take notes efficiently, avoid reading every source word for word. Instead, look through the table of contents and index of each book, skimming the relevant parts and focusing only on what pertains to your narrowed topic. Keeping your limited topic and purpose in mind will help you focus your search.

As you skim various sources, try to determine some key ideas or subtopics that you will use in the development of your paper. Use these ideas to make a rough outline. This outline will probably change while you research, but it is a useful starting point.

Note Cards

Take notes on 4" x 6" cards in order to distinguish these from your 3" x 5" bibliography cards. Because you will have to group your cards under separate topics in order to write your final outline and rough draft, use a separate card for each note. (Although writing more than one note on a card would save paper, it may in fact complicate your task. You may need one idea for the beginning of your paper and the other for the end of your paper. This would make sorting your material more difficult.)

Look at this sample note card for the Civil War paper. Then study the explanation of each part of the card.

Sample Note Card

Source Number

Guideline ——— Fears in Battle   4
Note ———————— Most soldiers feverish with
impatience before battle. Nothing
"brings . . . such crucial trial
as the throbbing emotions that
immediately precede the clash of
Page   arms."
Reference ——— 339

Here is an explanation of the parts of a sample note card.

12

1. The **guideline** is a heading that identifies the note on the card. The guideline corresponds to one of the key ideas on your preliminary outline. Include on the card only ideas pertaining to the guideline and use a different card for each source. If your reading does not yield enough information for your guideline, you may need to delete the topic from your outline and discard the corresponding note cards. If your reading yields new or different information, revise your outline and your guideline.

   As you work, you will probably want to keep cards with similar guidelines grouped together. You may even want to try to put the cards with similar guidelines in logical order. Of course, this order may shift as you learn more about your subject, but making the attempt to organize your notes as you work will simplify the task of ordering your material later on.

2. The **source number** corresponds with the number of your working bibliography card and stands for the source from which the note was taken. By checking the card in the working bibliography, you can obtain all the information on the source whenever needed.

3. The **page reference** must be exact for two reasons: (1) You may want to refer again to the source to verify the facts, and (2) you may need the page reference for documentation.

4. The **note** is the most important part of the card since it contains the information you will use in writing your paper. Except for direct quotations, all notes should be paraphrased.

Paraphrasing has two purposes. First, it helps you to take notes more quickly and efficiently. Second it helps you to avoid plagiarism.

Plagiarism

Because plagiarism is intellectually dishonest and is therefore a form of stealing, it is an extremely serious offense and can result in severe penalties, even a loss of credit for the course. All of these constitute plagiarism:

1. Failure to document with quotation marks any material copied directly from other sources
2. Failure to acknowledge paraphrased material (someone else's ideas)
3. Failure to provide a bibliography
4. Use of others' work as one's own, particularly in the arts
5. Use of others' ideas as one's own for themes, poems, musical compositions, or artwork

Improving Your Skill at Taking Notes

The following guidelines will help you improve your note-taking skills.

Effective Note Taking

1. Keep your topic, purpose, and audience in mind at all times. Do not bother recording material that is unrelated to your topic, that will not help you accomplish your selected purpose, or that is too basic or too technical for your particular audience.
2. Use indexes, tables of contents, glossaries, appendixes, and other parts of books to help you locate specific information.
3. Be accurate. Double-check statistics and facts to make sure you have them right. When you summarize or paraphrase a writer's words, be sure you do not misinterpret or distort the meaning.
4. Distinguish between fact and opinion. Label opinions: "Dr. Graves thinks that . . . " or "According to Grace Jackson. . . . " Be careful to note differences in opinion and to point out such differences in your notes.
5. Take notes as quickly as possible. Omit all word or phrases not essential to meaning. Use abbreviations when appropriate. Be careful, however, not to take notes so brief that when you need to use them again, you cannot understand what you have written.
6. Copy a direct quotation exactly from the source, including punctuation, spelling, and grammar. Be sure to use quotation marks both at the beginning and at the end of the quotation so that you can easily separate the quotation from the paraphrased material.
7. If you insert words into the text of a quotation, they must be enclosed in brackets ([ ]). Do not use parentheses in place of brackets. If your typewriter does not have a bracket key, insert brackets in ink.
8. Indicate the omissions of nonessential parts of a quotation by ellipsis points (. . .).
9. If you can't get all the information on one side of the card, write *over* in parentheses at the bottom of the card, flip the card over, and continue on the back. If you have more than two more lines on the back, you probably have too much material for one card.

Writing Activities   Taking Notes

A. In Part 3 you compiled a working bibliography for your own re-search paper topic. Now use that bibliography to prepare a rough outline for your topic.
B. As you prepare the rough outline for your research paper, you will also be working on a set of note cards for your topic. As you write your notes, be sure to follow the guidelines on page 14.

Part 5

Prewriting the Research Paper

Now that you have collected relevant facts and ideas, you are ready to begin the prewriting stage of your research paper. During this stage you refine your purpose, formulate a thesis statement, and organize your information into an outline.

Determining the Controlling Purpose

Your first step in the prewriting stage is to formulate a **controlling purpose** for your paper. This is a formal, exact statement of what your paper is going to be about. You began this process when you limited your subject. Now, based upon your reading and note taking, you can refine your purpose until it is clear and precise. You can use it to direct your drafting and any further research that might be necessary.

It is possible that you will want to revise your controlling purpose as you draft, but stating it as clearly as possible now will help you to select the right material from your notes. Material that does not relate directly to your controlling purpose does not belong in your paper.

For the paper on the Civil War, the writer is investigating the realism of the depiction of the common Civil War soldier in *The Red Badge of Courage*. While this provided a beginning, the topic could be more focused. Notice the rewording of this idea to provide a controlling purpose:

> ### One Student's Process
> Controlling Purpose: to demonstrate
> that Henry Fleming, the protagonist of
> Stephen Crane's The Red Badge of
> Courage, is an accurate portrayal of a
> Civil War soldier by comparing him with
> actual soldiers through their letters
> and diaries.

Writing a Thesis Statement

The controlling purpose serves as a working thesis statement during the planning stages of your research paper. It states the main idea, sets the tone, and indicates the direction your paper will take.

16

As you begin to write your paper, you may want to include a revised version of your purpose statement in the introductory paragraphs.

In the paper on the Civil War, for example, the writer begins the introductory paragraph with a general statement, explaining that American fiction often portrays the real-life experiences of a given historical period. Notice how the introduction ends with the following thesis statement, a revised version of the controlling purpose.

One Student's Process

Looking closely at a fictional character may thus provide the reader with a clear and accurate view of that character's era. Stephen Crane's novel The Red Badge of Courage presents such a view through the character of Civil War soldier Henry Fleming.

Organizing Your Material

Since a research paper is longer and more complex than a short composition, your outline will also be longer and more complex. Remember, however, that much of your work has already been done. The guidelines on your note cards reflect the divisions and subdivisions of your outline, which you have been modifying as you did research. Your next step is to organize these note cards so that you can write your first draft by referring to them.

Put each note card with the same guideline into a separate, distinct pile. You may already have begun this process during your research. Each of these piles should relate to one of the major or minor divisions of your preliminary outline. Study these piles of cards to see what information each contains. Also determine the extent to which the information conforms to the information on your preliminary outline. Refer to your controlling purpose often as you study your cards.

Gradually, some groups of ideas will emerge as major divisions of your subject, some as subdivisions, and others as sub-subdivisions. If some cards reveal insufficient material on a subdivision but you feel that the subdivision is important, you may have to do more reading. If the subdivision is not important, you can either combine it with another closely related subdivision or delete the information (and the card) entirely.

This is the point at which you decide exactly what you are going to include in your paper and what you are going to leave out. Keep checking your controlling purpose to see that all your usable material is relevant to your subject. Do not be afraid to delete information that is not relevant.

Finally, when you have chosen your main topics and subtopics and tested each note card for its relevance to your controlling purpose, begin to organize the topics for your final outline. Decide what order logically moves your topics toward the conclusion, which you have determined previously in your controlling purpose. Feel free to move an entire main topic from one place to another or to shift the note cards within a group to different positions.

Write down your main topics, ordering them in different ways. Next, study them, thinking about how to make logical transitions between topics. If a transition from one topic to another seems forced, something is probably wrong. Either you need to rearrange your topics or you need to revise the emphasis or the direction of one of them.

When you are satisfied with the order of your material, test it once more against your controlling purpose in the following ways.

Organizing Your Material

1. Have you organized your material so it begins at the beginning and moves logically to the conclusion?
2. Are the main topics the most important ideas?
3. Do the subtopics relate to the main topics?
4. Is there any unnecessary duplication?
5. Do all main topics relate clearly to the controlling purpose?
6. Are all transitions logical?
7. Does the conclusion correspond to the controlling purpose?
8. Is there too much information on any one idea?
9. Is enough information included to develop each idea?

When you are satisfied with the answers to these questions, you are ready to write your final outline.

18

Outlining the Research Paper

To begin your final outline, write down the major groupings and subgroupings in your devised order. Use standard outline form, as shown in the example below. Remember that a good outline is not necessarily a long, elaborate one. Study the following outline for the paper on the Civil War.

One Student's Process

I. A comparison of war experiences
  A. Memoirs of actual Civil War soldiers
  B. Experiences of soldiers in The Red Badge of Courage

II. Soldiers' attitudes toward battle
  A. Risks of combat
  B. Fear of cowardice
  C. Nervousness before battle
  D. Changing attitudes during battle

III. Problems of desertion
  A. Mental struggle
  B. Physical exhaustion
  C. Rationalization

IV. Differences between expectations and actualities of battle
  A. Physical
  B. Mental

V. Growing maturity of soldiers
  A. Coping with stress
  B. Attitude toward death

VI. The reality of war experience
  A. In the Civil War
  B. In The Red Badge of Courage

Writing Activities Prewriting

A. Read a magazine article on science or current events that is at least five pages long. Identify the article's controlling purpose and thesis statement (if one is stated). Then reread the article and try to write an outline similar to the one the writer might have used.

B. Write an outline for the research paper you have been working on throughout this chapter.

Part 6

Drafting the Research Paper

Writing a final outline is the last step in the prewriting stage of writing a research paper. You are now ready to begin work on your first draft. In this draft, do not worry about achieving an elegant style or about eliminating all errors in grammar, mechanics, and spelling. Simply attempt to get your ideas down in a form that you will be able to follow when you are ready to make revisions.

Follow your outline, and keep your controlling purpose in mind. Begin a new paragraph for every topic and subtopic on your outline, and attempt some transitions between and within paragraphs.

Write your entire paper in the third person. Never use *I, me,* or *my* because you will be in danger of injecting your own opinion, and personal opinion has no place in a research paper. The only opinions you should use are those of authorities. As was mentioned earlier, these opinions should be attributed to the authorities either directly or through a footnote. Use the information on your note cards as you write, and be sure to follow this information with the source number from the upper right-hand corner of your note card. You will need these sources for your footnotes. To save time, you can write only the first few words of a direct quotation in your rough draft. The source numbers will help you to locate the quotations quickly when you need to copy them carefully onto your final draft.

Stay alert to the possibility of using maps, charts, diagrams, and other graphic aids as a concise way to present some of your information. You can reproduce a graphic aid from one of your sources, or you can create one of your own. Just be certain to credit your source to avoid plagiarism.

As you write, keep in mind that the first paragraph of your paper will constitute your introduction, in which you set forth your controlling purpose. Your final, or concluding, paragraph should round up all your ideas in a restatement of your controlling purpose.

Writing from Your Outline

As you draft your paper, you will be using notes to expand on certain ideas and to supply appropriate examples. In doing this, you may begin to think about your main idea differently. You may find that you have more information on one idea than you first thought. You can change your outline to expand the amount of coverage on a certain point. In the paper on the Civil War, the writer had much more information about "changing attitudes during battle" (IId) than initially believed. The writer made that topic an entire division of the outline, deleted the topic from IId, and made it section III.

```
    III. Soldiers' change in attitude
         during battle
         A. Sense of urgency
         B. Feeling of rage
         C. Emergence of unity of purpose
            1. Abandonment of self
            2. Loyalty to army
```

Using Quotations

You will probably use a number of direct quotations in your paper. Be sure that these quotes fit into your writing smoothly and naturally. Include partial quotations, and those that are complete but brief, within the text of your paper.

> Roosevelt spoke of "the need to find a program that uplifts rather than degrades."

> The next step was to produce an airplane that could go faster than sound, but, according to Isaac Asimov, "There was talk of the sound barrier as though it were something physical that could not be approached without destruction."

Longer quotations—those of more than four typed lines—should be set off from the text. Indent the entire quote ten characters in from the left margin. Note that in this case no quotation marks are needed.

> In Psychology: A Biographical Approach, Malinda Jo Levin presents an interesting way of looking at dreams:

>> Recently it has become popular to talk of dreams in relation to creativity. Elias Howe supposedly perfected the sewing machine while in a dream state, and Robert Louis Stevenson dreamed complete stories.

In both long and short quotations, you should use ellipsis points to indicate deletions that are not relevant to your research paper. Use brackets when adding anything to a quotation—for example, when filling in the referent of a pronoun or clarifying a term that was introduced elsewhere in that source.

Documenting Your Sources

Any information you use from your sources must be documented, or credited to its original source. Documentation serves three basic purposes in your research paper:

1. To indicate the source of material that is directly quoted
2. To give credit for other people's ideas even though you write them in your own words
3. To give the sources of graphic aids, figures, or statistics

One commonly used form of documentation is the **footnote** or the **endnote**. The information to be documented by these notes should be numbered consecutively throughout the paper. Use Arabic numerals placed in the text of your paper, usually after the last word of a sentence or direct quotation. The note number should be placed slightly above the line on which it appears.

These notes may appear in one of two ways: at the bottom of each page (a footnote) or on a separate page at the end (endnotes). The form of each is the same.

If footnotes are to appear on each page, be careful to allow enough space at the bottom for all the footnotes on that page. Include a one-inch margin of blank space at the bottom of each page.

When you have typed the last line of text on a page, skip a line. Then type a line that extends across the page, from the left margin to the right. Skip another line, and then type your first footnote. Single-space the footnote, but double-space between footnotes. A footnote and its corresponding documentation look like this:

```
Sometimes, however, a forest fire may
actually play a useful ecological role in
preventing the buildup of excess brush and
debris, and also in allowing the development
of certain types of seeds.6
```

```
    6 René Dubos, The Wooing of Earth (New
York: Scribner's, 1980) 134.
```

For examples of standard footnote form and abbreviations used in footnotes, see Appendix A and Appendix B at the end of this book.

Parenthetical Documentation Currently, the most widely used and accepted method for citing sources is not the footnote, but a simplified method called **parenthetical documentation.** As explained in the latest edition of the *MLA Handbook for Writers of Research Papers,* this method lists the author's name and the page number from the source in parentheses after the paraphrased, summarized, or quoted material.

> Another private said "The knowledge of
> an impending battle always sent that
> thrill of fear and horror" (Capp 140).

If you use the author's name in the text when you make a particular point, your parenthetical documentation should include only the page reference.

> William Hinman echoed Henry's feelings,
> saying that a soldier had to "go
> through a struggle between his mental
> and physical natures" (398).

If you have cited more than one source from the same author, you should include the title of the source or a shortened version of that title after the author's name.

> He thought it better to "fall facing
> the enemy, than to play the coward"
> (Wiley, <u>The Life of Billy Yank</u> 68).

If you must include important information in the reference, place it within parentheses, after the direct reference to the cited material.

> According to one soldier, "If he shows
> the least cowardice he is undone. His
> courage must never fail" (Linderman 7;
> for a treatment of cowardice in <u>The Red
> Badge of Courage</u>, see Deitz 36-38).

Sometimes, a source in your bibliography will be attributed to a **corporate author,** such as the Department of the Treasury, the Environmental Protection Agency, or the United Nations Economic and Social Council. In such a case, use the corporate author in your documentation (Environmental Protection Agency 17) or simply mention the corporate author in the text.

At times, you will take information from an indirect source. That is, your immediate source will provide a quote from a second source. If the second source is not available, you may simply begin your parenthetical reference with the abbreviation *qtd. in* for "quoted in."

Compiling the Final Bibliography

Once you have completed the final drafting and documenting of your research paper, gather the bibliography cards for every source you have cited. You can use these cards to compile your Bibliography. The heading Works Cited may be used as an alternative to bibliography. If your list includes nonprint sources, then Works Cited is usually preferred. This list of sources displays the research you have completed and provides a list of references for the benefit of those who wish to investigate further. Sources that were not actually cited in the paper should not be included in the bibliography. The following guidelines will help you write a bibliography.

Compiling a Final Bibliography

1. Arrange all bibliography entries alphabetically by the last name of the author or editor.
2. If no author or editor is given, alphabetize the entry by the first word of the title. If the first word is *A, An,* or *The,* begin the entry with the second word of the title.
3. If you wish to do so, you may divide your bibliography into separate sections for books, magazines, and other sources. If you are following this procedure, each section should be separate and should begin with a subheading reading, in upper- and lower-case letters, Books, Magazines, or Other Sources.
4. Begin the first line of each bibliography entry at the left margin. Indent any subsequent lines within the entry five spaces.
5. Double-space each entry; also double-space between entries.
6. Place a period at the end of each entry.
7. Bibliography entries contain page numbers only when they refer to parts within whole works. For example, an entry for a chapter in a book or an article in a magazine should contain page numbers for the complete chapter or article.
8. Give shortened names of publishers for books. For example, Little is used as a shortened name for Little, Brown and Company. See pages 26-27 for more examples.

Basic Forms for Bibliography Entries

The following basic forms for bibliographic entries will help you when you need to cite sources with different elements.

Whole Books

A. One author
Webster, Charles. <u>From Paracelsus to Newton: Magic and the Making of Modern Science</u>. Cambridge: Cambridge UP, 1983.

B. Two authors
Gilbert, Sandra M., and Susan Gubar. <u>The Madwoman in the Attic: The Woman Writer and the Nineteenth Century Literary Imagination</u>. New Haven: Yale UP, 1979.

C. Three authors
Hepplewhite, Charles W., Jeannette M. Meyerhoff, and Gerhardt B. Kassenbaum. <u>The Effects of High Technology on Smokestack America: An Introspective</u>. Litchfield: Litchfield, 1988.

D. Four or more authors
Gatto, Joseph, et al. <u>Exploring Visual Design</u>. 2nd ed. Worcester: Davis, 1987.

Use *et al.*, Latin for *and others,* instead of listing all authors.

E. No author given
<u>Literary Market Place: The Directory of American Book Publishing</u>. 1984 ed. New York: Bowker, 1984.

F. An editor, but no single author
Saddlemyer, Ann, ed. <u>Letters to Molly: John Millington Synge to Maire O'Neill</u>. Cambridge: Harvard UP, 1984.

When you have cited several works from a collection, you may write one entry for the entire collection or list each work separately.

G. Two or three editors
Emanuel, James A., and Theodore L. Gross, eds. <u>Dark Symphony: Negro Literature in America</u>. New York: Macmillan, 1968.

Parts Within Books

A. **A poem, short story, essay, or chapter from a collection of works by one author**

Angelou, Maya. "Remembering." <u>Poems</u>. New York: Bantam, 1986. 11.

B. **A poem, short story, essay, or chapter from a collection of works by several authors**

Welty, Eudora. "The Corner Store." <u>Prose Models</u>. Ed. Gerald Levin. New York: Harcourt, 1984. 20-22.

C. **A novel or play from a collection under one cover**

Serling, Rod. <u>Requiem for a Heavyweight</u>. <u>Twelve American Plays</u>. Ed. Richard Corbin and Miriam Balf. New York: Scribner's, 1973. 57-89.

<u>The Red Pony</u>. <u>The Short Novels of John Steinbeck</u>. New York: Viking, 1963. 355-649.

Magazines, Encyclopedias, Reports, Newspapers

A. **An article from a quarterly or monthly magazine**

Batten, Mary. "Life Spans." <u>Science Digest</u> Feb. 1984: 46-51.

B. **An article from a weekly magazine**

Powell, Bill. "Coping with the Markets." <u>Newsweek</u> 27 Apr. 1987: 54.

C. **A magazine article with no author given**

"How the New Tax Law Affects America." <u>Nation's Accountants</u> 24 Sept. 1986: 66-69.

D. **An article from a daily newspaper**

James, Noah. "The Comedian Everyone Loves to Hate." <u>New York Times</u> 22 Jan. 1984, sec. 2: 23.

E. **An editorial in a newspaper**

"America and the Hypermarket." Editorial. <u>Chicago Tribune</u> 4 Jan. 1988, sec. 1: 10.

F. **An article in a journal that has continuous page numbers throughout the annual volume**

Lefkowitz, Mary R. "Patterns of Fiction in Ancient Biography." <u>American Scholar</u> 52 (1983): 209-10.

G. An article in a journal that numbers the pages of each issue separately

Aumiller, Emily P.   "<u>Lord of the Flies</u> as a
    Musical." <u>English Journal</u> 71.8 (1982): 32.
The volume number, the number of the issue, the date, and the
page number follow the title of the journal.

H. An encyclopedia article

"Western Frontier Life." <u>World Book</u>
    <u>Encyclopedia</u>. 1987 ed.

I. A signed review

Ludlow, Arthur. "Glass Houses." Rev. of <u>Rolling</u>
    <u>Breaks and Other Movie Business</u>, by Aljean
    Harmetz. <u>Movies</u> Aug. 1983: 76.

J. An unsigned, untitled review

Rev. of <u>Harry and Son</u>. <u>American Film</u> Mar. 1984: 78.

Other Sources

A. An interview

Farquharson, Reginald W.   Personal
    interview. 26 May 1988.

B. A letter that has not been published

Reagan, Ronald. Letter to Professor
    Stephanie R. Somerville. 22 May 1988.

C. A thesis or dissertation

Ortega, Miguel C.   "The Acceptance and
    Rejection of the American Dream: 1960 to
    1975." Diss., Southwestern Oklahoma
    State U, 1988.

D. Information in private files

Students of Paul D. Schriener. <u>Of Our Lives:</u>
    <u>A History of the 1960's and 1970's</u>.
    Dept. of Social Studies, Munster High
    School, 1981.

Writing Activity Drafting the Research Paper

Write a draft from the outline you created in Part 5. Use parenthetical documentation to cite your sources. Then, using the guidelines on page 25, compile a final bibliography for your research paper.

Part 7

Revising the Research Paper

After you finish drafting your research paper, the next step is revision. If possible, however, try to put the paper aside for a day or so. This process of "distancing yourself" from the paper can allow you to evaluate it more objectively.

Once you do revise your paper, read it through several times. Each time you can look for different problems. Reread first on a general level, taking the perspective of your audience. Ask yourself the following questions. Will the paper seem complete and logical to your audience? For example, is any crucial evidence missing? Or, conversely, are any of the existing elements repetitious or irrelevant? Do the ideas flow naturally from one to the next? Then revise for unity and coherence. Do your paragraphs follow each other logically? Are they linked with effective transitional devices? Do all the sentences within each paragraph fit together smoothly?

Now you can revise for smaller details. At this point, evaluate your writing style. Have you employed vivid and accurate vocabulary? Do you provide a variety of sentence structures and lengths to keep your reader interested?

Revising a Research Paper

1. Does your introductory paragraph engage the reader? Is it well developed? Does it set forth the controlling purpose of your research paper?
2. Does your paper follow your outline exactly? Is it well paragraphed? Do your ideas flow logically from one paragraph to the next?
3. Are your paragraph transitions natural and logical?
4. Does the conclusion of your research paper sum up your ideas and restate your purpose? Is it a logical result of what you wanted to prove?
5. Have you attributed all the ideas and direct quotations in the text and documented them correctly?
6. Have you tested the force and accuracy of specific words? Do you have interesting sentence variety?
7. Have you checked spelling, punctuation, and usage?

Finally, you can begin to proofread. After you have corrected all errors, make a clean copy of your paper.

Now read the final outline and copy of the research paper on the Civil War.

One Student's Process

The Realism of Henry Fleming
in Stephen Crane's
<u>The Red Badge of Courage</u>

I. A comparison of war experiences
  A. Memoirs of actual Civil War soldiers
  B. Experiences of soldiers in <u>The Red Badge of Courage</u>

II. Soldiers' attitudes toward battle
  A. Risks of combat
  B. Fear of cowardice
  C. Nervousness before battle

III. Soldiers' change in attitude during battle
  A. Sense of urgency
  B. Feeling of rage
  C. Emergence of unity of purpose
    1. Abandonment of self
    2. Loyalty to army

IV. Problems of desertion
  A. Mental struggle
  B. Physical exhaustion
  C. Rationalization

V. Expectations and actualities of battle
  A. Physical
  B. Mental

VI. Growing maturity of soldiers
  A. Coping with stress
  B. Attitude toward death

VII. The reality of war experiences
  A. In the Civil War
  B. In <u>The Red Badge of Courage</u>

The Realistic Portrait of Henry Fleming
in The Red Badge of Courage

American fiction often portrays the real-life experiences of a given period in history. Herman Melville's <u>Moby Dick</u>, for example, accurately depicts life on a whaling boat in the nineteenth century. Looking closely at a fictional character may provide the reader with a

Thesis statement

clear and accurate view of that character's era. Stephen Crane's novel <u>The Red Badge of Courage</u> presents just such a view through the character of Civil War soldier Henry Fleming. By examining the memoirs of Civil War soldiers and comparing them with Fleming's experiences, one can see that Stephen Crane's novel is an accurate portrayal of a soldier's emotions and actions during the war.

Key idea: comparison of war experiences

Henry Fleming, like many actual Civil War soldiers, feared the consequences of an impending battle. Henry thought that "as far as war was concerned he knew nothing of himself" (Crane 11). He also thought that "the only way to prove himself was to go into the blaze, and then figuratively to watch his legs to discover their merits and faults" (Crane 14). Many Civil War

soldiers had the same feelings as
Henry. Bell Wiley, a historian who has
done extensive research on the common
private of the Civil War, wrote that
soldiers were more concerned with the
question of how they would stand up in
battle than they were over the chance of
being wounded or killed (<u>The Life of
Billy Yank</u> 68). One private wrote, "I
have marked dread of the battle field,
for I . . . am afraid that the groans of
the wounded and dying will make me
shake. . . . I hope & trust that
strength will be given me to stand & do
my duty" (Wiley, <u>The Common Soldier of
the Civil War</u> 56; all first-hand
accounts cited are also in Dornbush).

Historian Gerald F. Linderman found

Key idea:
soldiers'
attitudes
toward war
concern with courage in the journals and
letters of soldiers (7). One said, "If
he shows the least cowardice he is
undone. His courage must never fail"
(Linderman 7; for a treatment of
cowardice in <u>The Red Badge of Courage</u>,
see Deitz 36-38).

This strong moral value, however,
produced some unexpected consequences.
The methods that some soldiers devised to
avoid battle or to alleviate their
doubts about their courage were many.
Some would self-inflict wounds; others

would leave the front on the pretense of
a broken musket, helping a wounded
comrade, being ordered to do some

Parentheti-
cal docu-
mentation
with title
special task by an officer, illness, or
a "call of nature." Many never returned
(Wiley, The Life of Billy Yank 86).

Like Henry, some soldiers tried to
relieve their fear of battle by
calculating the risks of combat. Before
the Battle of Perryville, three brigade
commanders discussed the chances of
their getting hit and of their troops
running. The generals predicted that
their troops would stay and fight and
that they themselves would not be hit,
but all three were killed and their
brigades were completely routed (Hillard
18). Like Henry's own calculations, the
officers' predictions were wrong.

This emphasis on courage served an
important purpose, according to
Linderman. The courageous soldier
believed that his "inner qualities"
would carry him through the "increas-
ingly depersonalized mass warfare"
(61). Many soldiers believed that the
courageous would survive and the
cowardly would die. Even in defeat a
soldier could be comforted by his own
courage (Linderman 61).

Many soldiers thus tried to hide

33

their true fears and go into the fight
as bravely as possible. One of these
real soldiers was Elbridge Capp. Like
Henry, who felt that he had to "go into
the blaze," Elbridge said to himself, "I
must face the danger" (Capp 135). Others
resolved to let death solve their problems. One of these soldiers said, "I'm
willin ter die . . . but I don't want
ter be no coward" (Hinman 400). Another
private, Sam Watkins, said, "I had made
up my mind to die" (234). Henry had
these same feelings, thinking "that it
would be better to get killed directly
and end his troubles" (Crane 225). He
thought it better to "fail facing the
enemy, than to play the coward" (Wiley,
The Life of Billy Yank 68).

The descriptions of Henry's
feelings immediately before and during
the battle were consistent with the
accounts of both Federal and Confederate
soldiers. Before facing fire for the
first time, Henry was in a fever of
impatience (Crane 24). Most soldiers
experienced this same feeling. One
wrote that nothing "brings . . . such
crucial trial as the throbbing emotions
that immediately precede the clash of
arms" (Hinman 339). Another private
said "the knowledge of an impending

battle always sent that thrill of fear and horror" (Capp 140).

Key idea: change in soldiers' attitude during battle

Once the firing started, however, Henry's feelings, as well as those of most soldiers, changed. Henry had been advised that a man changed in battle, and he found it was true (Crane 24). Before he went into action, Henry's main concern was for himself. After the battle opened, however, his outlook changed. "He suddenly lost concern for himself, and forgot to look at a menacing fate" (Crane 30). He became an automaton. Crane describes Henry's reaction as follows:

Use of block quotation

> He was at a task. He was like a carpenter who has made many boxes, making still another box, only there was furious haste in his movements. . . .

Parenthetical documentation with block quotation

> Following this came a red rage. He developed the acute exasperation of a pestered animal. . . . His impotency . . . made his rage into that of a driven beast. (31)

Civil War veterans' reminiscences echoed Henry's change from fear to indifference, rage, and urgency. One private wrote, "Strange as it may seem

to you, but the more men I saw killed
the more reckless I became" (Wiley, <u>The
Life of Billy Yank</u> 71). Henry Morton
Stanley, the famous explorer, wrote, "We
plied our arms, loaded, and fired, with
such nervous haste as though it depended
on each of us how soon this fiendish
uproar would be hushed" (354). Oliver
Norton, a Pennsylvania infantryman,
wrote, "I acted like a madman. . . . The
feeling that was uppermost in my mind
was a desire to kill as many rebels as I
could" (91). A third soldier, like
Henry, wished to grapple face to face
with his enemies: "I was mad . . . how
I itched for a hand-to-hand struggle"
(Wiley, <u>The Life of Billy Yank</u> 72).

Gradually, a feeling of unity--
oneness--with the army, the corps, and
the regiment manifested itself on both
the average Civil War private and Henry
Fleming. Throughout Crane's novel Henry
calls himself "part of a vast blue
demonstration" (10). When he first came
under fire, Henry experienced a feeling
common to many Civil War soldiers:

> He felt that something of
> which he was a part--a
> regiment, an army, a cause, or
> or a country--was in a
> crisis. He was welded into a

common personality which was
dominated by a single desire.
For some moments he could not
flee, no more than a little
finger can commit a revolution
from a hand. (Crane 30)

This same feeling was expressed by many
Civil War soldiers, Federals, and
Confederates alike. Bruce Catton, the
Civil War historian, argued that "the
instinctive loyalty of all these men
went . . . to the army" (360). Henry
Morton Stanley wrote that "there were
about four hundred companies like the
Dixie Greys, who shared our feelings"
(Commager 354). Sergeant Thomas H.
Evans, a member of the regular army,
said that an "abandonment of self"
emerged in battle (43). At the
surrender of the Army of Northern
Virginia, one private, "unwilling to
outlive his army," shouted, "Blow,
Gabriel, blow!" (Davis 40). Such
loyalties became more potent than the
cause for which the soldiers were
fighting (Crane 31).

On the other hand, flight from the
battlefield was not uncommon to Civil
War soldiers. In fact, "there was a
considerable amount of malingering,
skulking, and running in every

major battle" (Wiley, <u>The Common Soldier</u> <u>of the Civil War</u> 26). Henry Fleming's reasons for running were similar to those of many who fled from battle. When the Confederates charged for a second time, Henry ran. He saw "a revelation," and "There was no shame on his face" (Crane 36). A soldier in the Twelfth Connecticut was much like Henry. "He did not look wild with fright; he simply looked alarmed and resolved to get out of danger; . . . he was confounded by the peril of the moment and thought of nothing but getting away from it" (DeForest 63).

Soldiers who fled from the field of battle were generally beset with a conflict between their bodies and their souls. When the Rebels charged for the second time, Henry was exhausted and dismayed. "He seemed to shut his eyes and wait to be gobbled" (Crane 36). William Hinman echoed Henry's feelings, saying that a soldier had to "go through a struggle . . . between his mental and physical natures" (398). Hinman describes that struggle as follows.

The instinct of . . . [the physical nature] at such a time--and what soldier does not know it?--was to seek a

38

Use of
ellipses
place of safety, without
a moment's delay. To
fully subdue this
feeling by the power of
will was not . . .
such an easy matter as
might be imagined.
. . . some could never
do it. (398)

Soldiers who ran tried to
Use of
bracketed
information
rationalize their actions. Henry
described his flight from battle:

[He] was a little piece of the
army. He considered the time,
he said, to be one in which it
was the duty of every little
piece to rescue itself if
possible. Later the officers
could fit little pieces back
together again, and make a
battle front. If none of the
little pieces were wise enough
to save themselves from the
flurry of death at such a
time, why, then, where would
be the army? It was all plain
that he had proceeded
according to very correct and
commendable rules. (39)

Henry again tried to prove to
himself that he was right by "throwing a

pine cone at a jovial squirrel" (Crane 41). When the squirrel fled rather than let the missile strike him, Henry felt that "Nature had given him a sign" (Crane 41).

Actual combatants who ran from battle gave less symbolic, yet similar, excuses. A hospital steward stumbled on some skulkers at the Battle of Cedar Mountain and recorded the following:

> Some of these miserable wretches . . . muttered that they were not to be hoodwinked and slaughtered.
>
> "I was sick, anyway," said one fellow, "and felt like droppin' on the road."
>
> "I didn't trust my colonel," said another; "he ain't no soldier."
>
> "I'm tired of the war, anyhow," said a third, "and my time's up soon; so I shan't have my head blown off."
>
> (Townsend 493)

One soldier who deserted his comrades at the Battle of Corinth said on his return that he had not run, but had been detailed to guard a water tank. His comrades never let him live it down (Wiley, The Life of Billy Yank

87-88). Another soldier, nicknamed "Spinney," said he had run because he thought that the bullets were calling his name (Goss 197).

Whether they fled or fought valiantly, many soldiers were surprised by the realities of combat. At first, Henry "had the belief that real war was a series of death struggles with small time in between for sleep and meals" (Crane 10). He learned later, however, that battle took up very little time in a soldier's life (Crane 10). He also thought that "Secular and religious education had obliterated the throat-grappling instinct" (Crane 10). However, when the Confederates were

Incorporat-
ing
quotation
within
sentence

attacking for the first time, and Henry "wished to rush forward and strangle with his fingers," he realized that this thought was wrong, too (Crane 31).

Key idea:
differences
between
expectations
and
realities of
war

Many actual soldiers also experienced a difference between their expectations and the realities of battle. Henry Morgan Stanley wrote, "It was the first Field of Glory I had seen in my May of life, and the first time that Glory sickened me with its repulsive aspect and made me suspect it was all a glittering lie" (357). Sam Watkins wrote, "I had heard and read of

41

battlefields . . . but I must confess that I never realized the 'pomp and circumstance' of the thing called glorious war until I saw this" (42). Some were so naive that they were surprised that the enemy was firing bullets (Watkins 42; Stanley 353). This difference between the untrained soldier's image of war and the realities of combat was well portrayed in <u>The Red Badge of Courage</u>.

Under the stress of combat, both Henry Fleming and many actual Civil War soldiers rapidly matured. Henry's attainment of maturity was both quick and dramatic. Early in the novel, Henry felt the need to make excuses to escape the reality of his cowardice, but by the end of the book, Henry was able to look upon his feats, both bad and good, objectively. He thought that "He could look back upon the brass and bombast of his earlier gospels and see them truly" (Crane 109). Earlier, when Henry had been walking with a wounded soldier called "the tattered man," Henry felt guilty and embarrassed because he himself had no wound, while everyone around him had a "red badge of courage" (Crane 46). To escape his guilt and embarrassment, Henry ran from the

(margin note: Combining two sources in one reference)

(margin note: Key idea: growing maturity of soldiers)

tattered man, feeling that he "could
have strangled" his wounded companion
(Crane 52). By the end of the novel,
however, Henry realized that the
tattered man had actually been trying to
help him, and he felt guilty for
deserting this man who had cared for him
and aided him (Crane 108). When Henry
had outgrown the selfishness of
immaturity, he could finally say of
himself that "He was a man" (Crane 109).

Henry's attainment of maturity was
also common to many young soldiers.
Bell Wiley wrote, "One of the most
interesting things about the boy
soldiers was the speed with which they
matured under the stress and strain of
army life" (The Life of Billy Yank
301). Sam Watkins, a Confederate
private, wrote that early in the war "we
wanted to march off and whip twenty
Yankees. But we soon found that the
glory of war was at home with the
ladies, not upon the field of blood and
. . . death . . . I might say the agony
of mind were very different indeed from
the patriotic times at home" (21). One
soldier wrote the following:

> The new troops, they have not
> been called upon to train or
> restrain their nerves. They

are not only nervous, but they
blanch at the thought of
danger. . . . what to them,
on joining the service, was a
terrible mental strain, is
soon transformed into
indifference. (Holsinger 308)

This view of the experience of war
is also similar to Henry's. Before
Henry had attained his maturity, he was
nervous and afraid of how the strain of
battle and the thought of death would
affect him. After he had "become a
man," however, Henry could say matter-of-
factly that "he had been to touch the
great death, and found that, after all,
it was but the great death" (Crane 109).

Conclusion:
the real-
ities of war
Like many actual soldiers, Henry
gains a final understanding of the
meaning of life and death from his
experiences during the war. Henry's
diverse emotional experiences, his
growth to maturity and his eventual
feeling of unity with his comrades all
parallel the experiences that actual
Civil War soldiers had recorded in their
letters and diaries. These parallel
experiences reveal that The Red Badge of
Courage is an accurate representation of
real life under the conditions of the
Civil War.

Bibliography *

Books

Capp, Elbridge. <u>Reminiscences of the War of the Rebellion</u>. Nashua: Telegraph, 1911.

Catton, Bruce. <u>This Hallowed Ground</u>. Garden City: Doubleday, 1956.

Crane, Stephen. <u>The Red Badge of Courage. An Authoritative Text, Backgrounds and Sources of Criticism</u>. New York: Norton, 1976.

DeForest, John William. <u>A Volunteer's Adventures</u>. New Haven: Yale UP, 1946.

Dornbush, C. E. <u>Regimental Publications and Personal Narratives of the Civil War</u>. 2 vols. New York: New York Public Lib., 1967.

Goss, Warren Lee. "Yorktown and Williamsburg." <u>Battles and Leaders of the Civil War</u>. Ed. Robert V. Johnson and Clarence C. Buel. New York: Yoseloff, 1956.

Hinman, William. <u>Si Klegg and His Pard</u>. Cleveland: Hamilton, 1982.

Holsinger, Frank. "How It Feels to Be Under Fire." <u>The Blue and the Gray</u>. Ed. Henry S. Commager. Indianapolis: Bobbs, 1950.

Linderman, Gerald F. <u>Embattled Courage: The Experience of Combat in the American Civil War</u>. London: Free, 1987.

Norton, Oliver. <u>Army Letters</u>. Chicago: Deming, 1903.

The heading Works Cited may be used as an alternative to Bibliography. If your list includes nonprint sources, then Works Cited is usually preferred.

Robertson, James T. Civil War Books: A
    Bibliography. Baton Rouge: Louisiana State
    UP, 1967.

Stanley, Henry Morton. "Henry Stanley Fights
    with the Dixie Grays at Shiloh." The Blue
    and the Gray. Ed. Henry S. Commager.
    Indianapolis: Bobbs, 1950.

Townsend, George A. "A Camp of Skulkers at
    Cedar Mountain." The Blue and the Gray.
    Ed. Henry S. Commager. Indianapolis:
    Bobbs, 1950.

Watkins, Sam R. Company Aytch. New York:
    Macmillan, 1962.

Wiley, Bell Irvin. The Common Soldier of the
    Civil War. Gettysburg: Historical Times,
    1973.

---. The Life of Billy Yank. Indianapolis:
    Bobbs, 1951.

Periodicals

Davis, William C. "The Campaign to
    Appomattox." Civil War Times Illustrated
    Apr. 1975: 40.

Dietze, Rudolph. "Crane's Red Badge of
    Courage." Explorations Spring 1984: 36-38.

Evans, Thomas H. "There Is No Use Trying to
    Dodge Shot." Civil War Times Illustrated
    Aug. 1967: 43.

Hillard, James M. "You Are Strangely Deluded,
    General William Terrill." Civil War Times
    Illustrated Feb. 1975: 18.

Appendix A

Basic Forms for Footnotes

Whole Books

A. One author
[1] Margaret Mead, <u>Blackberry Winter: My Earlier Years</u> (New York: Morrow, 1972) 175-76.

B. Two authors
[2] Sandra M. Gilbert and Susan Gubar, <u>The Madwoman in the Attic: The Woman Writer and the Nineteenth Century Literary Imagination</u> (New Haven: Yale UP, 1979) 607.

C. Three authors
[3] Lois Jovanovic, June Biermann, and Barbara Toohey, <u>The Diabetic Woman</u> (Los Angeles: Tarcher, 1987) 14.

D. Four or more authors
[4] Gatto, Joseph, et al., <u>Exploring Visual Design</u>, 2nd ed. (Worcester: Davis, 1987) 17.

Use *et al.,* Latin for *and others,* instead of listing all authors.

E. No author given
[5] <u>Literary Market Place: The Directory of American Book Publishing</u>, 1988 ed. (New York: Bowker, 1988) 76.

F. An editor, but no single author
[6] Charles G. Duffy, ed., <u>Ballad Poetry of Ireland</u> (Delmar: Scholar's Facsimiles, 1973) 3.

G. Two or three editors
[7] Patricia Hill and Charlie Seeman, eds., <u>Folklife and Museums</u> (Nashville: American Assn. for State and Local History, 1987) 131.

Basic Forms for Footnotes

⁸ James Camp, X. J. Kennedy, and Keith Waldrop, eds., <u>Pegasus Descending: A Book of the Best Bad Verse</u> (New York: Macmillan, 1971) 14.

H. Four or more editors
⁹ Willard Thorp et al., eds., <u>The American Literary Record</u> (Chicago: Lippincott, 1961) 472.

The abbreviation *et al.* is Latin for the phrase *and others.* Use *et al.* instead of listing all the editors.

I. A translator
¹⁰ Albert Camus, <u>The Plague</u>, trans. Gilbert Stuart (New York: Modern Lib., 1965) 87.

J. Author, editor, and translator
¹¹ Andreas Capellanus, <u>The Art of Courtly Love</u>, trans. John J. Parry, ed. Frederick W. Locke (New York: Ungar, 1976) 42.

K. A particular edition of a book
¹² Donald Hall, <u>Writing Well</u>, 4th ed. (Boston: Little, 1982) 120-21.

L. A book or monograph that is part of a series
¹³ Marguerite C. Rand, <u>Ramón Peréz de Ayala</u>, Twayne's World Author Ser. 138 (New York: Twayne, 1971) 95-97.

M. A particular volume of a multivolume book
¹⁴ Francis James Child, ed., <u>The English and Scottish Popular Ballads</u>, 2 vols. (New York: Dover, 1965) 2: 17-19.

N. A volume with its own title that is part of a work of several volumes under a different title
¹⁵ George Holmes, <u>The Later Middle Ages: 1272-1485</u>, vol. 3 of <u>A History of England</u>, ed. Christopher Brooke and Denis Mack Smith (New York: Norton, 1966) 57.

Basic Forms for Footnotes

Parts Within Books

A. **A poem, short story, essay, or chapter from a collection of works by one author**

[16] Randall Jarrell, "The English in England," The Third Book of Criticism (New York: Farrar, 1969) 287.

When the name of the author of the work appears in the title of the collection, you may omit the first mention of the author's name:

[17] "Hamlet and His Problems," Selected Essays of T. S. Eliot (New York: Harcourt, 1964) 122.

B. **A poem, short story, essay, or chapter from a collection of works by several authors**

[18] Alberto Rubio, "Portrait of a Little Girl," New Voices of Hispanic America: An Anthology, ed. Darwin J. Flakoll and Claribel Alegría (Boston: Beacon, 1962) 94.

C. **A novel or play from a collection of novels or plays published under one cover**

[19] Rod Serling, Requiem for a Heavyweight, Twelve American Plays, ed. Richard Corbin and Miriam Balf (New York: Scribner's, 1973) 300.

If the author of the collection is mentioned in the title of the collection, omit the first mention of the author's name:

[20] The Red Pony, The Short Novels of John Steinbeck (New York: Viking, 1963) 356.

D. **An introduction, preface, foreword, or afterword written by the author of a work**

[21] Peter R. Limburg, preface, Stories Behind Words (New York: Wilson, 1986) 13-14.

E. **An introduction, preface, foreword, or afterword written by someone other than the author of a work**

[22] Harry T. Moore, preface, Palimpsest, by Hilda Doolittle (Carbondale: Southern Illinois UP, 1968) viii.

Basic Forms for Footnotes

Magazines, Encyclopedias, Reports, Pamphlets, and Newspapers

A. An article from a monthly or bimonthly magazine
[23] Mary Batten, "Life Spans," <u>Science Digest</u> Feb. 1984: 49.

B. An article from a weekly magazine
[24] Douglas Davis, "Art in the Marketplace," <u>Newsweek</u> 30 Jan. 1984: 67.

C. A magazine article with no author given
[25] "Challenging Mount Etna's Power," <u>Time</u> 30 May 1983: 48.

D. An article from a daily newspaper
[26] Noah James, "The Comedian Everyone Loves to Hate," <u>New York Times</u> 22 Jan. 1984, sec. 2: 23.

If no author is given, begin with the title. If the paper is divided into sections, include the section number or letter before the page number.

E. An editorial in a newspaper
[27] "The Politics of Arms Control," editorial, <u>Chicago Tribune</u> 29 Jan. 1984, sec. 5: 2.

F. An article in a journal that has continuous page numbers throughout the annual volume
[28] Mary R. Lefkowitz, "Patterns of Fiction in Ancient Biography," <u>American Scholar</u> 52 (1983): 209-10.

G. An article in a journal that numbers the pages of each issue separately
[29] Emily P. Aumiller, "<u>Lord of the Flies</u> as a Musical," <u>English Journal</u> 71.8 (1982): 32.

The volume number, the number of the issue, the date, and the page number(s) follow the title of the journal.

H. An encyclopedia article
[30] "Architecture," <u>World Book Encyclopedia</u>, 1983 ed.

Basic Forms for Footnotes

I. A signed review

[31] Arthur Ludlow, "Glass Houses," rev. of <u>Rolling Breaks and Other Movie Business</u>, by Aljean Harmetz, <u>Movies</u> Aug. 1983: 76.

J. An unsigned, untitled review

[32] Rev. of <u>Harry and Son</u>, <u>American Film</u> Mar. 1984: 78.

If the review is unsigned but has a title, use the form for a signed review but delete the author's name.

K. A report or pamphlet

[33] American Medical Association, <u>Medical Relations Under Workmen's Compensation</u> (Chicago: American Medical Assn., 1976) 3.

If the report is by an individual author rather than by an association or committee, begin with the author's name.

Other Sources

A. An interview

[34] E. Talbot Donaldson, personal interview, Sept. 1978.

B. A letter that has not been published

[35] E. D. Hirsch, Jr., letter to the author, 22 May 1988.

C. A quotation

[36] Robert Benchley, as quoted in Alistair Cooke, <u>America</u> (New York: Knopf, 1973) 273.

D. A film

[37] <u>Gandhi</u>, dir. Richard Attenborough, Columbia Pictures, 1982.

E. A work of art

[38] Paul Klee, <u>Twittering Machine</u>, Museum of Modern Art, New York.

Basic Forms for Footnotes

F. **A television or radio program**
[39] "A Desert Blooming," writ. Marshall Riggan, <u>Living Wild</u>, dir. Harry L. Gorden, prod. Peter Argentine, PBS, WTTW, Chicago, 29 Apr. 1984.

G. **A musical composition**
[40] Frédéric Chopin, Waltz in A-flat major, op. 42.

Subsequent Reference Footnotes

To refer to sources already cited, use a shortened form.

A. **In most cases, the author's last name, followed by the relevant page numbers, is sufficient.**
[41] Susan Sontag, <u>Illness as Metaphor</u> (New York: Farrar, 1978) 50.
[42] Sontag 79-80.

B. **If references by other authors with the same last name are used, include the author's first name or initials.**
[43] Edmund Burke, <u>Reflections on the Revolution in France</u>, ed. Thomas H. D. Mahoney (Indianapolis: Bobbs, 1955) 30.
[44]Kenneth Burke, <u>The Philosophy of Literary Form: Studies in Symbolic Action</u> (New York: Random, 1957) 21.
[45] Kenneth Burke 77.

C. **If more than one work by the same author has been referred to, you should write the author's last name and the title. The title may be in shortened form.**
[46] Will Durant, <u>The Pleasures of Philosophy: A Survey of Human Life and Destiny</u> (New York: Simon, 1953) 179.
[47] Will Durant, <u>The Story of Philosophy: The Lives and Opinions of the Great Philosophers of the Western World</u> (New York: Simon, 1961) 209.
[48] Durant, <u>Story of Philosophy</u> 49.

Appendix B

Reference Words and Abbreviations Used in Footnotes

Here are some of the more common reference words and abbreviations used in footnotes. Some of these words and abbreviations are no longer used in writing footnotes and bibliography entries, but are provided here for reference.

bk., bks.	book or books
ca. (or c.)	*circa*, "about" or "near." Used with approximate dates: ca. 1776; "ca." is preferable to "c.," which can also mean "chapter" or "copyright."
cf.	*confer*, "compare." Used, for example, when you wish to have your reader compare footnotes 22 and 23, which follow: cf. footnotes 22 and 23 or cf. *Ernest Hemingway, The Sun Also Rises,* p. 15.
c., ch., chs., (or chap., chaps.)	chapter(s)
col., cols.	column(s)
comp.	compiled or compiler
ed., eds.	editor(s), edition(s)
e.g.	*exempli gratia,* "for example"
esp.	especially (as in "pp. 208-232, esp. p. 220")
et al.	*et alii,* "and others"
et seq.	*et sequens* and *et sequentes,* "and the one following," "and those that follow." But cf. "f.," "ff."

ex., exs.	example and examples
f., ff.	and the following page(s) or line(s). These abbreviations are replacing *et seq.*
fig., figs.	figure(s)
fn.	footnote (Cf. "n.")
ibid.	*ibidem,* "in the same place"; i.e., the single title cited in the note immediately preceding.
idem	(no period; sometimes *id.*) "the same." Used in place of ibid. when the footnote is to the same source on exactly the same page as that referred to in the note immediately preceding.
i.e.	*id est* "that is"
illus.	illustrated, illustrator, illustration(s)
l., ll.	line, lines
ms.	manuscript
mss.	manuscripts
n. or nn.	note or notes (as "p. 48, n. 2")
n.b., N.B.	*nota bene,* "note well"
n.d.	no date
no., nos.	number(s)
op. cit.	*opere citato*, "in the work cited." If several different items have come between the first mention of a book and a subsequent reference to it in a footnote, the last name of the author is repeated, followed by *op. cit.* and the page number.

p. or pp.	page(s)
par., pars.	paragraph(s)
pass.	"throughout the work, here and there" (as pp. 79, 144, *et passim*)
pref.	preface
pseud.	pseudonym, a pen name: e.g. Mark Twain, pseud.
rev.	review, reviewed; revised, revision
sec (or sect.), secs.	section(s)
ser.	series
sic	"thus, so." If the word *sic* in brackets [sic] is inserted in a quotation, it shows that you are recognizing and pointing out an error or a questionable statement. For example: "There were nine [sic] men on the bench at that time." Your own additions to quotations are shown by bracketing those words added: "He [Wouk] was a member of the New York Writers' Club."
st.	stanza
trans. (or tr.)	translator, translation, translated ("by" understood in context)
vol., vols.	volume(s)
vs.	*versus,* "against"; also verse

INDEX